# Making Simple Kites

## CHRIS WOOD

STUDIO VISTA
LONDON

A Studio Vista book published by
Cassell & Collier Macmillan Publishers Ltd
35 Red Lion Square, London WC1R 4SG
and at Sydney, Auckland, Toronto, Johannesburg
an affiliate of
Macmillan Publishing Co. Inc.

New York

ISBN 0 289 70688 2

Printed in Great Britain by
Hazell Watson & Viney Ltd, Aylesbury, Bucks

# CONTENTS

To make the octopus kite you need:
a postcard, tissue paper, curtain ring,
string, paints or crayons, glue.

**Trace the octopus onto a postcard.**
**Then paint it.**

6

**2** Cut eight 1cm (or ½in) strips of coloured tissue paper.
Make each strip ten times the length of the card.

**3**

Glue the strips in a row at the bottom of your postcard.

**4** With a needle, make a small hole in each corner of the postcard.

**5**

A ————————————

C ————————————

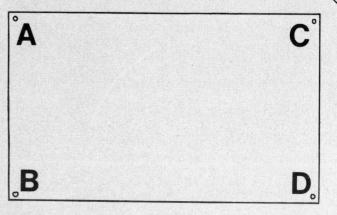

Cut two pieces of string. Make one the same length as line A–B, the other the same length as line C–D.

Thread one end of string A–B through hole A, and tie it. Then thread it through hole B and tie the end. Thread one end of string C–D through hole D. Finally thread the string through hole C and tie it.

Where the two strings cross, tie them together with the end of the long string with which you are going to fly the kite.

A

C

B

D

B

D

# Snake Kite

Make the snake kite in the same way as the octopus kite. But only use one tail. Make the tail as wide as the card. Paint the snake's head on the card.

You need: paper, a ping-pong ball, string, Sellotape, glue, a small curtain ring and paints or crayons

Make a large paper cone. It should be big enough to wear as a hat. Sellotape it together.

**2** Trim off the point, so that you have a small hole of about 1cm (or $\frac{1}{2}$in) across. Glue a thin strip of card or stiff paper round the wide end of the cone to strengthen it.

**3**

Make four holes in the card edge. Space them out evenly.

Ask a grown-up to make two 1cm ( ½in) holes in the top and bottom of a ping-pong ball, using a sharp knife or a hot knitting needle.

5

Dab glue round one of the holes in the ping-pong ball. Push it onto the end of the cone.

ear

Trace this shape and cut out two of these shapes for the ears.

With a needle, make several small holes in the mouse's nose, near to the ping-pong ball. Tie a knot in one end of some short lengths of string. Put a blob of glue on each knot and thread the string through the holes. These are the whiskers.

Glue the ears onto the mouse.
Paint the nose and ears.
Draw on a mouth and eyes.

**9** Cut four pieces of string. Make each one about 30cm (or 1ft) long.

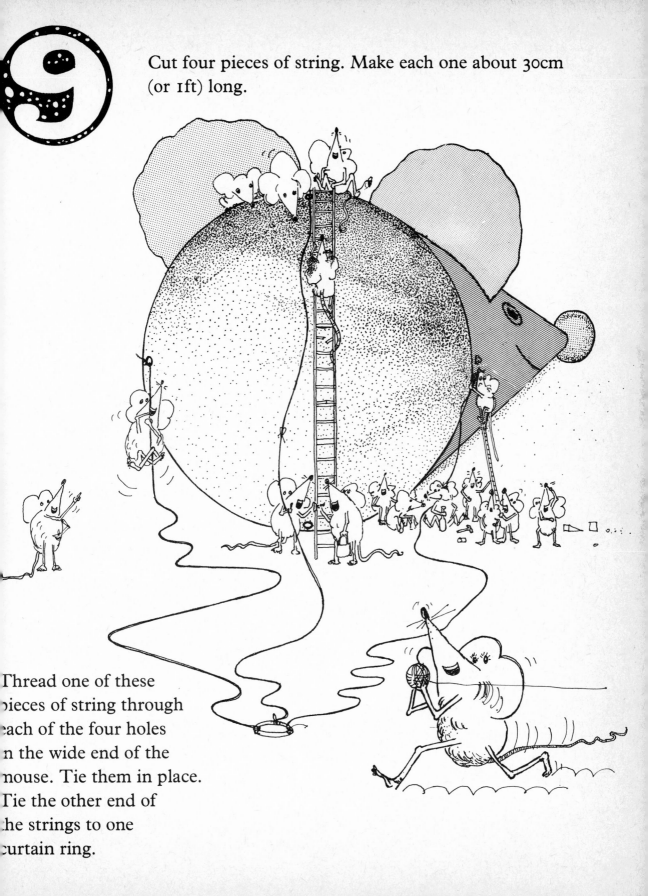

Thread one of these pieces of string through each of the four holes in the wide end of the mouse. Tie them in place. Tie the other end of the strings to one curtain ring.

# Dragon Kite...

To make the dragon kite
you need:
a sheet of stiff cardboard
coloured tissue paper
paints or crayons
string or strong thread
a curtain ring
scissors and glue

This is quite a difficult
kite to fly. The more
sections you make it with,
the harder it becomes.

This dragon has only six
square sections. You could add
some more when you become
really good at flying it.

Draw a large square on your card and cut it out with the scissors.

Cut out five more squares
Make each one
smaller than the one
before. The largest square
will be the face.

Make a hole in each corner of all the squares with a blunt needle.

To measure the length of one string bridle, wind a piece of string four times round the largest card. Now cut three more pieces of string the same length.

Tie one end of all four pieces of string to a curtain ring. Then thread the string through the holes in the corners of the squares.

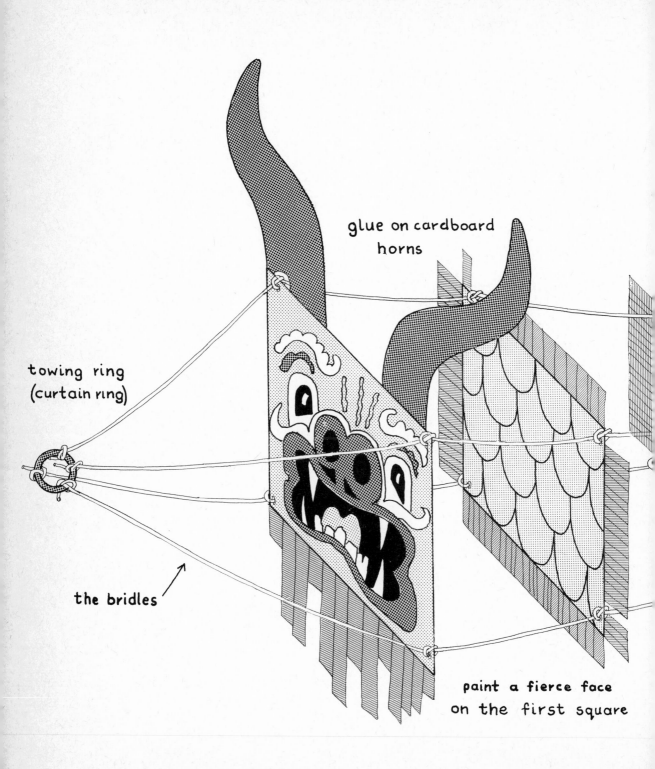

glue on cardboard
horns

towing ring
(curtain ring)

the bridles

paint a fierce face
on the first square

Tie a knot round each corner to keep the squares apart.
Leave a space the length of two sides of the largest square
between the ring and the first square. Leave a space the
length of one side of the largest square between the
squares.

you could glue
tissue paper tails to
the corners of each
square

glue on fringes (see page 36)

CLOWN

You need: paper or thin card, glue, two lolly sticks, string, paints or crayons, a blunt needle, and a curtain ring

fold lines

Trace this outline onto a sheet of stiff paper or thin card. Then cut it out. Draw the dotted lines onto your outline.

Bend the kite along the dotted lines so that when you look at it from the end it looks like this.

Without snapping them, gently bend each lolly stick in the middle.

Glue the lolly sticks across the fold in the kite. Do not close up the fold. Leave a gap under the middle of each stick.

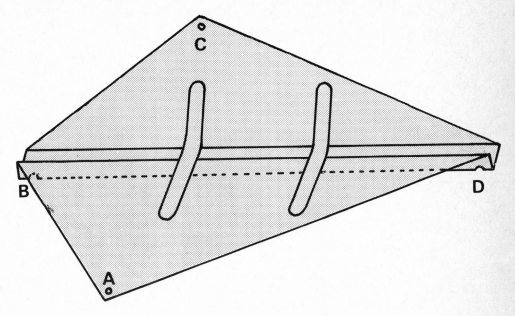

Cut a piece of string long enough to reach from A to B to C.
Make a hole with a large needle at A and at C. Tie one end of the string to A. Then tie the other end of the string to hole C.

Cut another piece of string long enough to reach from B to C to D.

Make a hole with a large needle at D and at B. Tie one end of the string to B. Tie the other end to hole D.

Where the strings cross tie them together with
a small piece of string.

The clown does not need a tai
to help it fly. But you could
attach a small tail made of
tissue or crêpe paper for
decoration.

Now paint a clown's face
on the kite.

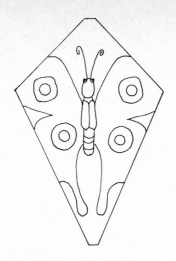

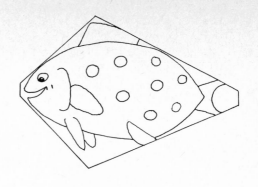

You could change your clown into a ghost.

Glue the kite onto a large sheet of white tissue paper. Trim off the areas which are shaded in the diagram. Cut along the dotted lines. This will make lots of streamers.

Make a Red Indian from the same kite too. Glue a long strip of white paper to the lefthand point, and one to the righthand point. Glue paper feathers, or real ones, down the strips and along the top edge. Draw in a face and add some war paint.

This is a hang glider ski kite. On the next page you will find out how to make a hang glider kite which you can throw like a paper aeroplane or fly like a kite.

You need: four balsa wood sticks all the same length, a curtain ring, tissue paper, glue and string

You can make a bigger triangle
than this one.
But the angle at **X** must be
the same as the one marked here.

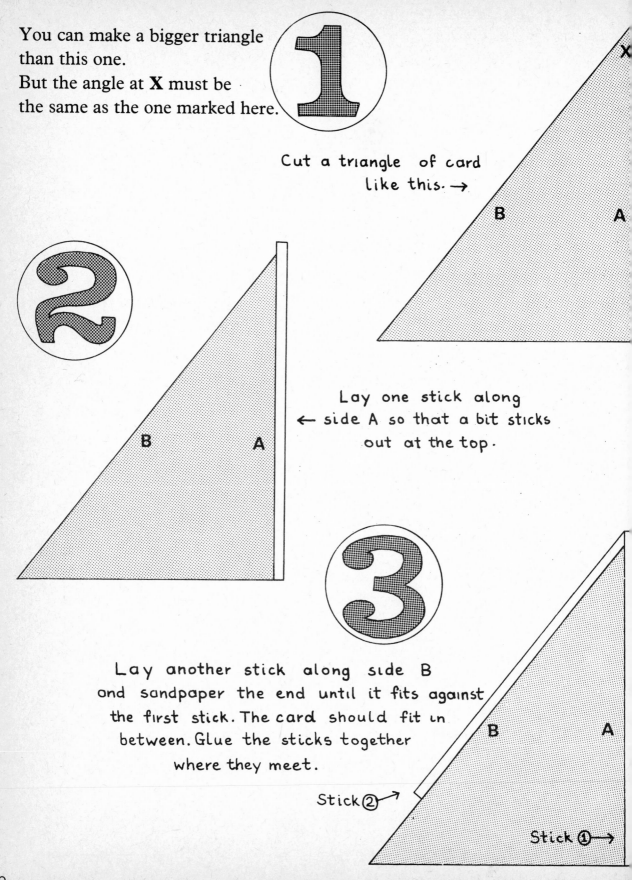

Cut a triangle of card
like this. →

Lay one stick along
← side A so that a bit sticks
out at the top.

Lay another stick along side B
and sandpaper the end until it fits against
the first stick. The card should fit in
between. Glue the sticks together
where they meet.

Stick ②↗

Stick ①→

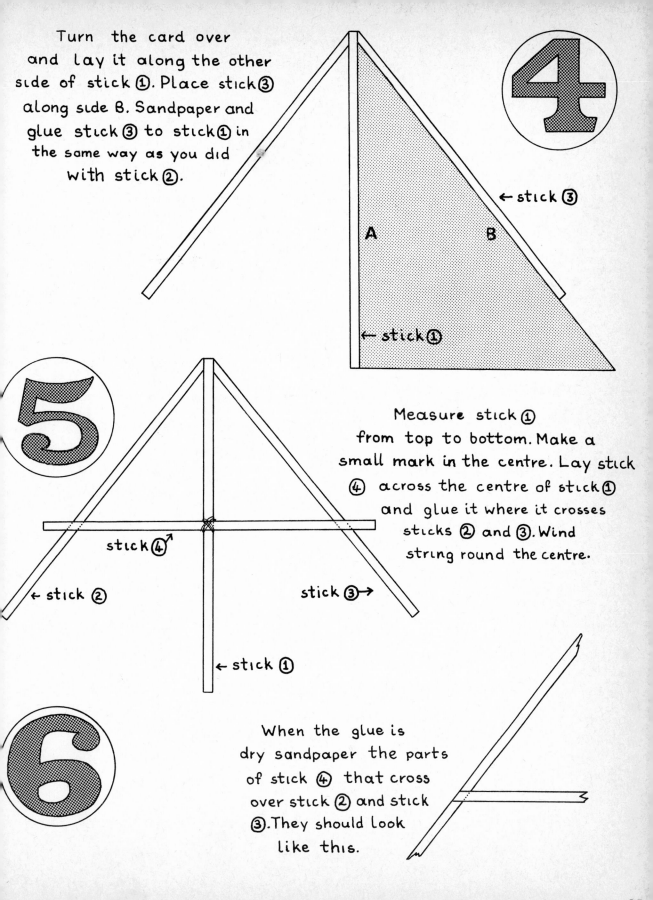

Turn the card over and lay it along the other side of stick ①. Place stick ③ along side B. Sandpaper and glue stick ③ to stick ① in the same way as you did with stick ②.

**4**

← stick ③

A          B

← stick ①

**5**

stick ④ ↗

← stick ②

stick ③ →

← stick ①

Measure stick ① from top to bottom. Make a small mark in the centre. Lay stick ④ across the centre of stick ① and glue it where it crosses sticks ② and ③. Wind string round the centre.

**6**

When the glue is dry sandpaper the parts of stick ④ that cross over stick ② and stick ③. They should look like this.

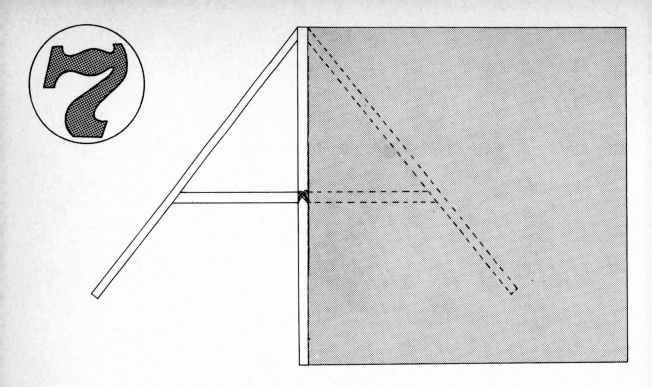

Next cut a square piece of
tissue paper. Make it the
same length as the middle stick.

Fold it corner to corner.
Make a crease along the fold.
Then open it out flat again.

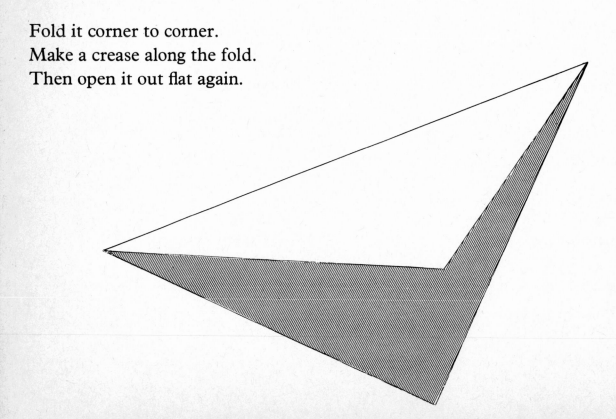

**8**

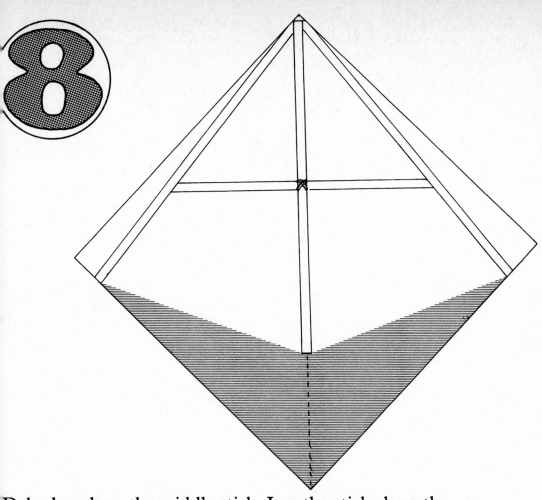

Dab glue along the middle stick. Lay the stick along the crease in the tissue paper. When the glue is dry, trim off the area which is shaded in the diagram. Dab glue along the sides of the side sticks. Allowing the paper to curve slightly, press the edge of the paper against the glued sticks.

To make the bridles, cut two pieces of string the length of A to B. Tie the end of one piece at B, the other at C. Then tie both pieces to a curtain ring. Cut a piece of string the length of A to D. Tie one end at A and tie the other to the curtain ring.

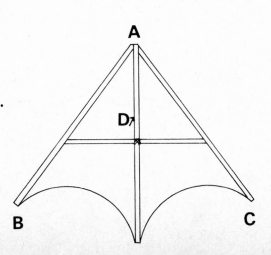

# HOW TO DECORATE YOUR KITE

*Tails*

The simplest kind of tail
is a long strip of paper;
you can decorate it with
coloured paper, milk bottle tops,
streamers, pieces of wool,
thin ribbon, or any light,
colourful material.

Many kites need a tail to keep them flying straight. If the kite is small and light it will need a light tail. If it is heavy, it will need a longer, heavier tail. When you go out to fly your kite, always take an extra piece of tail with you to add to the kite if it needs it.

You could make a rainbow tail. Glue pieces of different coloured tissue paper across a sheet of plain paper. Then cut it into strips and glue the strips end to end.

You can make a tail by tying strips of paper, ribbon or cloth to a piece of string. Or you could thread milk bottle tops onto the string. Tie a knot between each top to keep them apart.

## Kite

You can paint or stick pictures or patterns on the kite.
Tissue paper fringes, streamers and paper curls can look
very decorative too. Or you could even cover the whole
kite with silver foil.

To make a fringe, take a wide strip of paper, and make
lots of cuts from one long edge almost to the other.

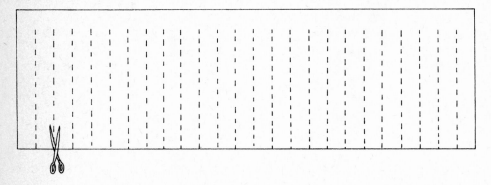

To make paper curls, you need long thin strips of paper.
Either roll them tightly round a knitting needle for a few
seconds, or pull them gently between the edge of a ruler
and the table.

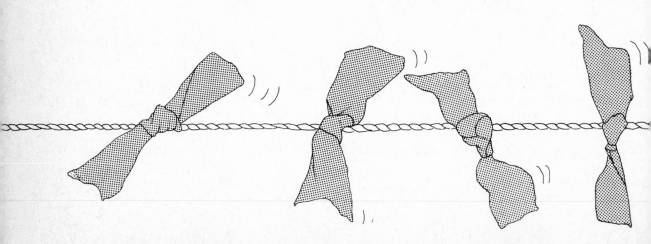

You can make paper streamers or even paper tails more interesting by snipping patterns out of them. Fold the streamer or tail like a concertina. Then snip out the pattern and open out the paper. The pattern will cover the whole streamer or tail.

Why not make a chain of paper girls or boys to trail from your kite? Fold a long strip of paper to and fro.

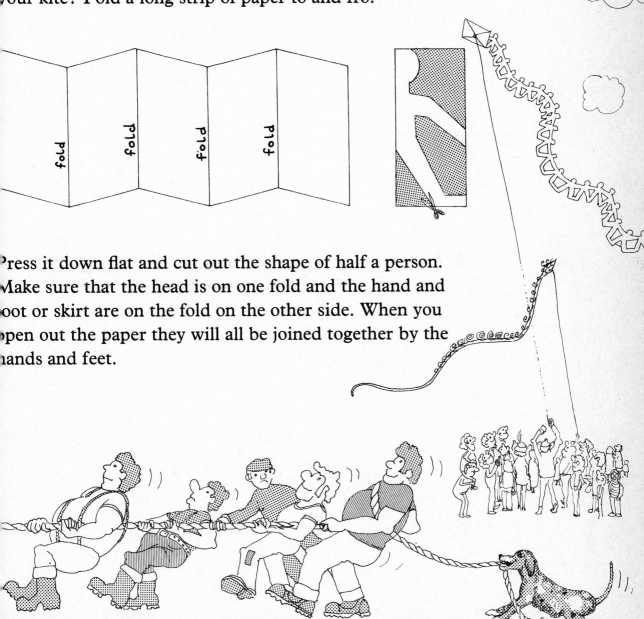

Press it down flat and cut out the shape of half a person. Make sure that the head is on one fold and the hand and foot or skirt are on the fold on the other side. When you open out the paper they will all be joined together by the hands and feet.

# how to fly your kite

Choose a day when the wind is steady,
but not too strong. Stand with your
back to the wind. Ask a friend to stand
in front of you and hold the kite
tilted into the wind. If you are
by yourself, hold the kite at arm's length
by the curtain ring. When the wind lifts the
kite, gently let out some line.
Do not let the line out too quickly.

To help the kite rise, hold the line
at arm's length. Then gently pull it back,
and let it out again. Allow more line
to slip off the reel as you do so.
Do this gently and smoothly.

If the kite moves towards the left,
or towards the right, you should
follow it. If it suddenly dives sideways,
quickly let out more line.

If the kite falls to the left,
or to the right, add a small
weight, such as a paper clip, to
the opposite side.

If it will not rise, then the
tail is probably too heavy.
If it dips and thrashes, then
it needs a heavier tail.

To land your kite, choose a clear spot where there is
nothing in the way. Slowly wind in the line. If the wind
is strong, walk towards the kite at the same time.
If you have a helper with you, he can hold the reel
while you put your hand over the line and slowly walk
towards the kite as it gradually comes down.

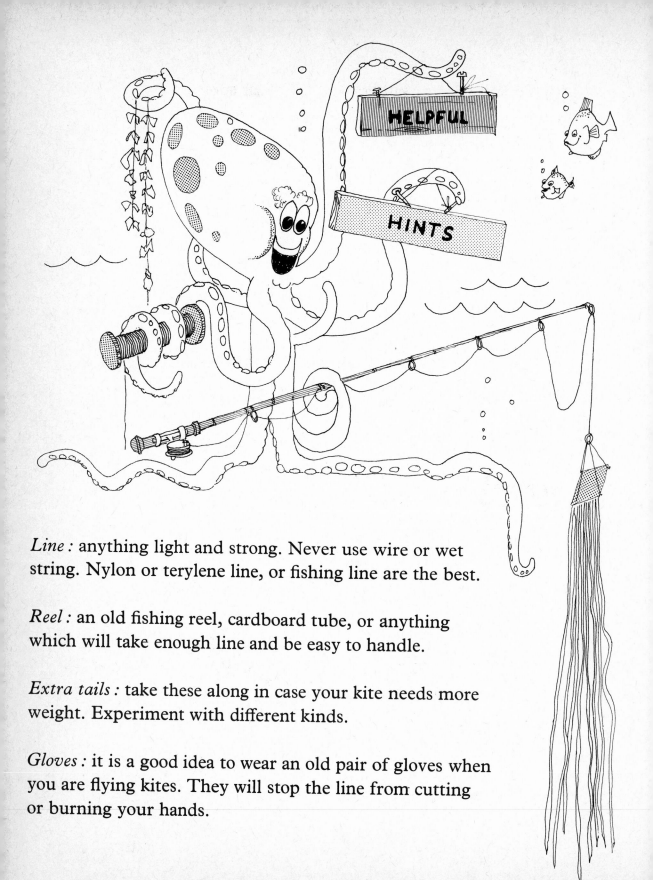

*Line :* anything light and strong. Never use wire or wet string. Nylon or terylene line, or fishing line are the best.

*Reel :* an old fishing reel, cardboard tube, or anything which will take enough line and be easy to handle.

*Extra tails :* take these along in case your kite needs more weight. Experiment with different kinds.

*Gloves :* it is a good idea to wear an old pair of gloves when you are flying kites. They will stop the line from cutting or burning your hands.

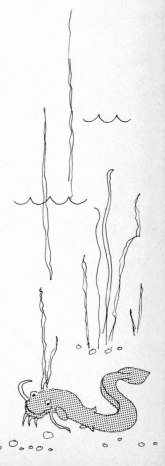

**Don't** fly your kite when the wind is very strong, or near trees where it could get caught—you will lose it.

**Don't** take risks trying to get a lost kite back. It is much easier to make a new one than to be badly hurt.

**Don't** fly your kite in thunderstorms or near electric cables. You could be electrocuted.

**Don't** fly your kite near main roads or railways. A runaway kite could cause a serious accident.

**Don't** fly your kite near airfields, or too high. In Britain you must be at least five kilometres (four miles) from an airfield. You must not fly your kite over sixty metres (two hundred feet). If you do then you will be breaking the law.

**Don't** walk backwards without knowing what is behind you.

# Index